MAURICE RIORDAN
Floods

ff

faber and faber
LONDON·NEW YORK

First published in 2000
by Faber and Faber Limited
3 Queen Square London WCIN 3AU
Published in the United States by Faber and Faber, Inc.,
an affiliate of Farrar, Straus and Giroux, New York

Photoset by Wilmaset Ltd, Wirral
Printed in England by MPG Books Ltd,
Victoria Square, Bodmin, Cornwall

© Maurice Riordan, 2000

Maurice Riordan is hereby identified as author
of this work in accordance with Section 77
of the Copyright, Designs and Patents Act 1988

A CIP record for this book
is available from the British Library

ISBN 0–571–20462–7

2 4 6 8 10 9 7 5 3 1

i.m. Bina Twomey

Time is what keeps everything from happening at once.
Chaos for Beginners

Acknowledgements

Thanks are due to the editors of *Heat* (Australia), *Independent on Sunday*, *Last Words* (Picador, 1999), *London Review of Books*, *Pivot* (US), *Poetry Island*, *Poetry London Newsletter*, *Poetry Wales*, and *Voices* (Australia), where some of these poems were first published; and to the BBC's *Stanza* and *Poetry Please* programmes, where some were broadcast. 'Badb' was written for Ted Hughes's sixty-fifth birthday and appeared in *A Parcel of Poems* (Faber and Faber, 1995). 'Southpaw' and 'Caisson' were prizewinners in the 1996 and 1998 National Poetry Competitions respectively. 'The Boy Turned into a Stag' retains phrases from, and is otherwise indebted to, Kenneth McRobbie's translation of Ferenc Juhász' 'The Boy Changed into a Stag Cries out at the Gate of Secrets'. The lines of Ovid recalled in 'Floods' are adapted from Ted Hughes' *Tales from Ovid* (Faber and Faber, 1997). I am grateful to the Arts Council/An Chomairle Ealaíon, the Society of Authors, and the London Arts Board for financial support.

Contents

The Sloe

That he died alone in the gully
below the pass in a snowstorm, the first
of the year, in a lurch of the seasons
which became a change of climate;
that he died some three to five weeks
after an assault – from a wild beast
or fellow man – which shattered
his ribcage and sent him above
the tree-line, far from the settlements,
that he died really from
being alone, an injured man
relying on his few resources – which were,
however, both innate and military,
so that he carried about him
not only weapons and tools
but spares, medicine, and a sewing kit,
fire, and the means of fire,
and was observant and skilled
about stone, wood, grasses, skins,
about stag-horn and bone – knew for each
its properties and use, but he died
like Xenophon's comrades on the trek
home through Armenia, as soldiers
have died on all recorded
winter marches, not from lack of discipline
or the body's weakness, or not only,
but because of the slight
shortening of the odds which comes
with the unexpected comfort of snow;
so that prepared for the next day's climb,
his equipment in order,

the backpack, the axe, the two
birch-bark containers, one holding
tinder and flints, the other
insulated with damp sycamore leaves
(but no longer carrying live embers),
the quiver, and beside it the straight new bow
with its unused string, the bird net
spread, the pannier upright,
he ate the last of his food
– all except, oddly, a sloe –
then lay on his uninjured side
in the best available shelter
and pillowed his head, while the snow
(which would lull and warm him)
spiralled out of the night and marked,
as I've said, a change in the Tyrol,
a climatic glitch which lasted 5,000 years
until the thaw on the glacier two summers ago
brought him to our attention,
then here to the Institute;
so that, although I can tell you
nothing of his gods or language,
almost nothing of his way of life,
whether he was shepherd, headman,
or shaman, the last of his village
or employed on some delicate embassy;
whether he moved in the forest
among spirits and shades
or was himself almost a shadow
who with a visceral roar
fell on a victim and bludgeoned
his brains, whether on a raid
he would satisfy his need with a woman or child

[2]

or, contrariwise, was himself
husband and father,
a tender of flocks in the epoch
of transhumance: gregarious, hierarchical,
a transmitter of geographical lore,
of trails, cloud changes, windbreaks,
who sang at the camp fire –
though I can tell you nothing of this
I can tell exactly
how he died, how in his plight
he couldn't string the green yew stave,
he couldn't ignite the tinder
to roast the songbirds
and, from the decalcified traces
on the humerus, I can tell
he kept, those last weeks, one arm
crooked, in a virtual sling,
thus giving the broken ribs time
to knit (as indeed they were doing)
and can guess, in the interim, he hoped
for an Indian summer of nuts, mushrooms, fruit,
a fire not quite dead,
even a maggot-ridden carcass;
and for a hand with the bow stave
he would have given in exchange his knife
or his coloured tassel with its marble bead,
that one inutile item polished
so spherical and white
it seems, like the sloe,
extraneous ... but everything
comes down to the sloe, the uneaten sloe:
herders from Anatolia to the Ötzal,
even to the present day, pick

[3]

these sour, purplish almost pith-less fruits
and, like my Grandfather Bögelmann
when he dropped one in his fob,
they say 'A frost will sweeten it'
– so it is grave goods, viaticum,
food for the soul on its journey,
in its flight from the tip
of the punctured heel or the slit
tattooed into the lumbar,
and when the temperature drops
and the body's anaesthetized,
as the brain sinks into its reverie
of log fires and song,
of dripping fat and tree sap,
even as the skin adheres to the earth,
the tannins and acids disintegrate
so that now, as I put the sloe back in the ice,
I tell you it is edible,
that, by morning, it was sweet.

Frost
after Seán Ó'Ríordáin

I found a hankie on the whitethorn
outside in the freezing cold this morning.
When I reached up to get it, it slipped –
or skipped? Anyhow it missed my grip.
Not just a sprightly rag, I thought,
more like 'something' died out here last night ...
As I sought the right analogy
this surfaced in my memory:

>   The kiss I gave my cousin
>   before they covered her coffin.

The Cemetery Expansion

Like two reluctant armies, the new graves
advance from either end of the field. Soon,
next year I think, they are going to meet
and find they're the one army after all.

My Birthday

Invariably a card arrives
(surfer airborne above a roller,
or goggled chap in sports car);
then, under separate cover,
a thoughtful bit of folding.

But not this year. Neither.
I worry: now she's really old,
on her own, maybe out of sorts.
Then she phones: quite unperturbed,
chatty, unwary of the cost.

It was on account of Easter
being so late, she says. You were
my Easter egg, did you know,
born Easter Sunday? Yes, I knew!
But was it in the morning?

I hear a mocking *ha*. Not at all,
it was late, between four and five.
You were breech, y'know, and took your time.
I still hear the midwife's words:
Thank God, at least he's alive.

Badb

I was walking where the woods begin
with an almost sheer drop to the river
– so that I was eye level with the tops
of nearby trees and higher than the branch
when I came upon the crow sitting there,
so close I could have touched her with a stick.
She was creaturely and unwary, as the wind
bore her away and brought her back.
We shared the same tangy woodland smells,
the same malt-pale October sunlight.
Then I must have made a sound,
for she came alert and looked at me.
And, in that interval before the legs
could lift her weight from the branch,
as the beak sprang open to deliver
its single rough vowel, she held me off
with a look, with a sudden realignment
of the eyes above the gorping mouth.
It is the look known to legend and folk belief
– though also an attribute useful for a bird
without talons or guile to defend it.
Then she was gone, in a few wing beats
indistinguishable from her fellows wheeling
above the trees, carrying on their business,
neighbourly and otherworldly.

The Comet

Asked what the chances were to find, in a life of observation,
another comet, either Hale or Bopp replied, Astronomical!

*

The comet was travelling in the north-western sky,
with a semblance of its explosive speed stilled
as in an action-photo, the months you were dying.
It accompanied the plane over and back, forth and back.
It was there, above the tree, when I went outside to smoke.
There as I feigned sleep in my nephew's room next door,
Ryan Giggs life-size in football gear above the bed.
There, though I didn't mention it, the night you chafed
my trouser leg, and called for mirrors, lights
– when Margaret softly came to cajole you into prayer
and, as the damaged pathways fired, you took off
into the Joyful Mysteries, decade after decade,
the *Memorare*, Hail Holy Queen – a voice young
and agile, the drover's mantra against alcohol
and trouble that had once brought us to our knees
before dances, dates. I expected you to die,
I expect I wanted you to die, that night.
Time stopped, it slid or swerved. Yet it must have kept
as well the comet's stately pace. Some things
happened in my life, yet they didn't happen.
The world of work, friends, of closer ties, subtly changed,
or changed with violent shifts. I can't say when
I looked at the sky and told myself *It's gone*,
nor the day I woke to find a space clear in my head
and I thought *Yes, I can start to look again.*

The Rug

The small boy has abandoned his game
with the rolled-up tinfoil ball. He's rolled back the rug
to expose the newspapers placed there as underlay,
is absorbed now in action-photos and bold-print reports
of hurling matches: the sticks swing, the oiled horseskin
flits in the clear blue behind his eyes,
the roar almost reaches him from the terraces,
from the Athletic Grounds, Semple Stadium, Croke Park
– Cork's glorious summer
the summer before he was born.
When, in a minute, his mother's face appears round the door,
What's that you're doing?, what will he say,
whatever shall I say as I look up at her for the first time?
That we overlap but we do not coincide,
all this before I was born ... I have dipped my feet
in the cold element, it rears up to the heavens,
somehow it hasn't crashed onto the good rug,
the play things, the vase on the inlaid mahogany,
a dark-green fish carrying a silk flower in its mouth.
The boy will say nothing. He has no word
for the sickness in his stomach. He helps
his mother. Together they'll put the papers back,
smooth the rug down with their feet. She'll tell him,
It cost twenty pounds – more than you cost!, how the
    shopgirl said
newspaper would take up the damp, and she'll admonish him
Not to go doing that again, like a good man.

The Boy Turned into a Stag
after Ferenc Juhász

A mother calls to her only son
    across the distances.
She comes to the front of the farmhouse
    And calls out to her son.
She undoes the silver coil of her hair,
it falls loose like a wedding veil to her waist;
the filaments catch the last of the summer light,
the bloodstain of the sky above her shoulder;
it catches photons from the stars; her face
exchanges its reflection for the moon's.
She calls to her son (as she was wont to do
when he was a small boy) in a sing-song voice,
sending her summons out over the hedge,
the potato-rows, the frills of white flowers,
over the bank of rushes, over a herd
of grazing somnolent bullocks; sending
her words to eels in the bog-holes, to fleeting
diesel-rings on puddles, launching her voice
high into the wind now, into lark song
and cloud whisper, the humming power lines,
among sudden peewits, the winter geese.

    Bird and beast, flowers of the field
        Listen, hear me
    Fish of the alkaline lakes, vermin
    Worm and parasite, pollen wandering
    The air tunnels, enzymes and sugars
        Listen, I cry out

Glands of the earth, forest and river
You phantoms, colour and strange
Whirring in the spaces of the atom
       Listen, I cry out
Acids and salts, chromosomes
When you weave – clockwork, cascade –
Then ravel the chain-dance of harvest
Amoeba, virgin and constellation
       Listen, hear me!

I have gone blind in this world of surfaces.
My shins are scarred, my eyes are bruised green-and-yellow.
The universe rushes at me from all sides: the chair-leg,
the gatepost butt me with their horns; doors and windows
    jam,
the electric kettle shoots me with its volts; my sewing scissors
scuttles off my lap, the matches hop like wagtails' feet;
the pail handle nips at me like a cornered rat.
I'm no longer the sprightly doe in her motherly pride
who ran with you on her back to the schoolhouse.
Varicose veins have erupted on my legs, and my feet
glister with bony calluses; my finger joints crackle
with arthritis, and my skin is spotted with scales.
I'm all amort with inner lights. They dart into my head
from my body which is like a sick and fretful child.
I am startled awake in the night: I see the cockerel
in a crowing fit on the wash line, among men's shirts
which have bellied out and frozen stiff from the wind.
       Come home to me, son.
Straighten things out for me; sort the forks
from the combs, the fuses from the clothes pegs.
For all I am now are two gritty green eyes
lidless and glassy like the *libellula*'s.

Do you remember it? – how it used to engross you!
Two crystallized pippins in its green-lit skull
– that's me now, staring at the world
as though I no longer belonged to it.
Come home to me, son, exhale your smoky breath
into the air and set the place to rights again.

Asleep in the woods the boy heard.
His head jerks as he tests the air
in his nostrils, then listens dead-still
as he would to the huntsman's step
or the first dry-cough of sticks
when fire starts in the underbrush.

He breaks cover, breasting through
nettles, rushes, moon-shadow,
his spine softening with sweat.
He clears a rotted tree-trunk,
then clambers headlong down
the rock face to the silver lake,

and there lowers his head
to the water: the shifting backdrop
of the oaks, and among them
the sweat-mask of his face,
the flared slant of his skull
with its tree-shape of antlers

branching out, breaking into
leaflets among dark matter
and the stars. Terror
and memory build in his neck,

as he strains for an answering cry.
Nothing comes but a dull bell.

He kicks at the mirror of water,
then stoops as the shadows regroup
and again the stag's head forms
in the foam-light of the moon.
But now the boy's voice comes
like melt-water, treble and clear.

My footsteps won't be heard again inside the house.
I live now in sun-curtained corridors, among
Moist airs and oestrous smells, on a finicky diet.
I nibble tender shoots of wet young grass, I eat
First growths, coumarin-scented clovers, woodruff,
The melilots. Or I take dusky mast from the oaks.
I rise with the ease of the athlete from his bunk.
I wear my buck horn the way Uncle Julius wore,
Remember, his sombrero when he drove to town.
Like a young mother lifting her dream-heavy son
From his cot, or a reggae guitarist who shakes
His locks above the dance floor, such is my poise,
Such the adrenaline in my blood – when I shimmy
And dart through the beech groves, when I play
With shadows, the strobing shaft of the moon.

> *You speak like a stag*
> *a hounded stag, my woodland son*
> *When the hunter's horn*
> *the mass bells sound in the crystal air*
> *When fields turn green*
> *brown to green with seedling corn*

Don't you recall
the martins' nest by the feed-house door
Don't you remember
hide-and-seek with the orphaned foal
When wood pigeons call
near and far off the wood pigeon calls

Do you not remember how you came running in
from school, all agog about your latest class report?
Or the tawnies you kept in the water butt, the hare
you trapped and sold for a shilling, or the toad
you dissected and dried on the windowsill; how,
days on end, you patiently built plastic aeroplanes;
or the maps you drew, of the whole world, freehand –
with its rivers, mountains, lakes, in different inks?
Do you not remember your sweetheart? The priest
who taught you to sketch? How your own father
taught you to ride the mares – saddle and bareback?

A cold wave has broken over all of that,
all my childish things. Who knows what's happened
to the sketching priest with the orchid mouth?
Mother, don't mention my father.
He'll rise from his grave, his nails
and hair will start to grow, he'll collect
his yellow bones and come staggering out.
I remember the day Williams the undertaker
came with his soapy face, tut-tutting and pointing
this way and that, saying you take the feet,
steady on now, while my stomach turned,
and we fitted father into the coffin.
Then my own brother-in-law, the barber,

shaved him. I touched father's hair.
It was alive, oily and black, still growing,
ready to fill out the beard on his chin,
to overgrow the coffin lid, to spill
from the room, entangling the candles,
the lights in the yard, the stars in the forest pools,
then the constellations themselves,
while our local woman-chorus
stood around, saying their rosaries.
Outside the white wicket the hearse purred,
barely turning over, as the wipers
swept the windscreen and rain soaked
the mourners. When we lifted him in
the hand brake slipped and the driver swore,
then the brass band struck up, all his old cronies
playing him out of the yard forever,
playing for the card-games, the late nights
in darkened pubs, the fair days and mart days,
days at point-to-points, drinking in the marquees,
the days following the hunt, the women who cursed
and rode side-saddle; the good harvests, the wet,
the loft dances and ploughing championships.
And he led them, saying *Play up, boys*,
and they played, with fingers like fat
ballerinas, their Adam's apples hopping
as though they drank down bottled pints
to quench the thirst and sweat of the years.
No – he's history now, my father.
His brains lie rotting in the earth
like a sliced tuber ready to sprout.

Gentleness entered the hand
Of the boy who ran by the hedgerow
Who stood chest-deep in the river
And heard the sob of the starling
Who watched his father and uncle
Cutting the foal from the mare
Who saw the candle light flutter
On the violet lips of the dying

The wind has coarsened the laugh
Of the boy perched on the hay load
Who clung to the neck of the foal
The wind has roughened the hand
And grief bewildered the boy
Aloft with the telegraph wires
Who bent at night to the pond
Stealing crystals from starlight

There he stood, bleeding and serene, his antlers
hoisted among the stars, bolted to the roof-beam
of the world as he rode the toppling wave of time,
the stag-boy, radiant at the gate of secrets.
Yes, I am wounded a hundred times a day
The countless cells in my body die
And instantly they jump to life again
My wounds bleed fire and molten gold
Diamonds harden in the lava of my arteries
My antlers rise like pylons brandishing electricity
My eyes are the figured mirrors on the satellites
My tendons the cabling of office towers
My nerves the interstices of the city at night
My testicles are the sun and the moon

The marrow in my bones was expelled from the stars
My brain exfoliates among the foaming galaxies
I hum with the universe in my veins.

Stag of the electrified forest, boy-groom
To the pixel screen, the accurate flight path;
The blind voyeur in the benzene dawn;
The obliging courteous moon-jockey
Moping through night's stinking cordage;

Hide in the bracken, sniff the wind's radar;
Listen now for the loosened elm's low moan;
Crawl into the dead air of the bridge arch,
Sink one foot, then another into seepage,
Hearing the light's click in the foliage;

Females have taken you in thrall
They prey at your ear and smile to the mirror;
They've spun you telephonic silken threads,
And bound you with their soft duplicities.
    Son, come home. The eyes
of the *libellula* cannot rest till you come.

When the blood jets from the neck,
when he staggers out of the oak shade,
when the muscles flood with adrenaline
and the forelegs buckle under the branches,
then he will come, lanced and humiliated,
from the tournaments of light. He will come
with the sun to his left, the moon on the right,
to the toll of the bells, the crunch of the wheel rut,

bending under the power lines – lost to the hunt
and warm with lead shot, carrying the hayseed.
Then you will lay me out in my old room,
your old-woman's hands will strip me naked,
you will wash my sores, my love-wounds and time-scars,
you will bless my balls with spittle and close these eyes.
You will sprinkle my skin with water from the butt.
And when the flesh has swelled and broken open,
when it putrefies, it will sweeten again in the flowers.
I will lick from the stoup of your blood,
I'll clamber over the carbons of your stomach.
I'll become once more the tree in your womb.

Bilberry

Never having yet uttered a word
I race out of the barley field and lift
the horse-head knocker from the blank door.
Beyond, my aunties Jo and Kit are plotting
the orchard, while Godfather Uncle Ned
goes on his knee, *one foot in the grave/*
the other in Heaven, to edge the scythe.
He runs a wet thumb along the blade

when the knocker slips and sinks
through the oak; the whole barley field emits
a groan as it falls to the sickle's single stroke,
the orchard trees come down in a rain
of pitch black blossoms,
and my hand comes to my cheek,
comes to the three days' stubble on my cheek.

The Edwardian Tea-Taster

I don't suppose it's the sort of thing I'll find
on the Portobello Road, if indeed its like
was ever made: this perfect Edwardian gent
in a frock coat and puce velveteen trousers,
with a minuscule real cane, top hat, silks;
the whole design complete down to brass and pewter
fitments, and fiddly gas ducts – now cut off,
for it seems the device has been electrified.

And still works! As I discover when I tip
some used leaves ineptly in its warming jug,
and thereby set in motion an arm that lifts
a tepid spoonful to the taster's lips
– at which he bends double, sputters, spits;
generating all around (and from above?) a chorus
of soft laughter: a moist throaty utterance
I can't, for several seconds, get a hold of,

then wake with it bubbling from my lips, the sound
already dispersed; and now verifiable
only by an odd, and oddly intimate,
disarrangement of the muscles of my face
– that, plus a willingness, hours early, to get up;
to make tea the way our Grandmas did:
a patient, hot, viscous infusion, then served
(*why thank you, little man!*) very nearly black.

The Lettuce

I gave the barrow-girl two quid for it,
a frisée lettuce, a wild intricate wheel,
nature's very own bright-green mandala.
A lot of money but I paid up gladly,
even though at that time, anxious and overtired,
I parted most weeks from something: my bike
hitched to a loose railing; then gloves, umbrella,
wallet, cards, glasses – all left on the train.
I came to think of it as tribute: a mean,
but bearable, percentage exacted by
my personal Luck-god, who'd bring us through
that winter, and the next. So I paid up,
grateful to reach my own front door,
to enter a house at peace and register
that palpable all's well, before I swapped
briefcase and shopping for two small bodies.
I rebuke him now only for that one green
Mediterranean thing departing from me,
days before Christmas, for the Kent coast.

Silk

Should I tell you that just a century ago,
in the year of my father's – your granddad's – birth
the distribution of the silk industry
stretched as far as Tiverton to the west
and north to the looms and tenements of Paisley,

or that when, technically, silk is *thrown*
a single filament which is drawn unbroken
from the cocoon can measure a kilometre or more
and so, in this, it shares a subtle topology
with the network of veins beneath the skin,

which when stretched across, say, your collar-
or your pelvic-bone will reveal the bluish hues
of *Bombyx mori* eggs when they're freshly laid;
and since your skin has something too of the texture,
even the smell, of shantung and raw tussore

must I not then repeat to you the words of Count
Dandolo who, in his treatise on sericulture,
wrote of the worm itself: 'the greater the heat
in which it is hatched, the greater are its wants,
the more rapid its pleasures, the shorter its existence'?

On Not Experiencing the Ultraviolet Catastrophe

Unlike my childhood neighbour Jacksy Hickey
Who, rain or shine, wore a black gabardine,

Reasoning what was good to keep heat in
Was good enough, by definition, to keep it out,

We, when we reach the heart of the cornfield,
Know better: we shed each other's clothes.

Oh, you are radiant, my dear, and I am hot for thee!
But what, you ask, is heat? This I claim to know ...

Then I tell you why a tea cup doesn't scorch
And why, for instance, Josiah Wedgwood's kilns

Only baked Black Country clays to lucent jasper
With the help of an unknown hand: the constant *h*

Blocking frequencies in the ultraviolet range
And which, according to our century's laws,

Is true even to the cosmic radiation coming
At us, year on year, from the origins of time.

A modest number, with its dairy herd of noughts
After the point, it almost is – but isn't – zero.

By its mercy, we lie in the face of heaven.
You may lie beside me flesh to flesh. For this

You may be shunned, you may turn a dusky porcelain.
My love, you may be skinned. But you will not burn.

Caisson

If light, then, could part the carbon lattices

Or: our ears were like bats' – but so enhanced,
So threaded into the brain, we saw the world

As noise: the tearing of skin, or keratin,
Hand abrading hand, would reverberate

Along 'the hearing bones' and be resolved
As line, texture, colour. We could view

Our neighbours eating lunch or in their pool,
While our furthest vista might be the ocean

Or a vestigial wave-roar from the galaxies.
And as we went about our weekday lives,

In windowless rooms and vehicles, in our almost
Soundproof business suits (that reflected back

A low-toned humming), we'd have modes of dress
Devised for the open air, for sport and beachwear,

And cunning fabrics to tease and startle with.
Then, at your undressing, I would be

Plunged in a runic chemistry, in the
Liquid densities, the folding geometries.

And love itself would be a coming back
From the depths, from the labyrinthine mass

To the simple contour; and when our pitched breaths
Dodged/collided, as they amplified or cancelled out

Each other, we'd cry not for these sore truths,
But for surfaces and the amnesty of light.

Caroline Songs

I

Even as your hand undoes my shirt
    I believe you tell me lies,
Even if you mean to cause no hurt
    When you make those eyes / *disguise*

As your hand begins to reassure
    And my body shakes for you,
Even though I can no longer care,
    I believe it's true / *untrue*

Even as you make the sounds of love
    You slip inside the mirror,
And no word or gesture can remove
    The silver terror / *error*

II

When you sport the orange kepi
All I know is you are happy.

When you try the satin toque
I see I'll have to stretch my luck.

When you wear the Russian felt
I think I see the mark of guilt.

Then you don the black fedora,
And I know it all will soon be over.

III

The late-night take-out eats,
The mid-coital puff,
Cigarette burns in the sheets
  – My dear, I liked it
When you said you liked it rough.

The airborne Weetabix,
The mobile phone's rebuff,
That item in my letterbox
  – I said I liked it
When you said you liked it rough.

The hair-pull, pinch, the bite,
The experimental cuff,
Monosyllables of the night
  – My dear, I liked it
When you said you liked it rough.

I sink upon one knee,
I offer you my scruff,
Now treat me to the irony
  – I said I liked it
When you said you liked it rough.

IV

When you came to me warm,
When you came to me lonely,
You brought me no harm,
When you came to me only.

Just come again once,
It'll make it less lonely.
Oh, it might bring us peace.
Just come to me only.

v

You were nice to sleep with when nothing much occurred.
    Sometimes you gave a nervous laugh
    Or at some fierce endearment stirred;
    Sometimes, let's say, you gently snored
While one strong leg across my lower half
        Kept me ensnared.

But you were nice to sleep with. You never turned
    And from my word I never swerved,
    Bewildered by the trust I earned
    Or else, let's say, the fear I learned
When your long leg around my middle curved
        And I burned.

While like a child you slept, who into danger spied;
    Who once some darkened landing risked
    Or found night's sweating mares untied;
    Who once, let's say, had taken fright
At gentle damage, of love a question asked
        And been denied.

We seldom met with friends,
The photos went untraced,
And the hours and hours of phone-calls –
The tapes have been erased.
So what's the damage, love, where the harm?

The bus goes past your window,
It's lost its singing driver.
The pub has changed its décor,
Someone else enjoys the cider.
So what's the damage, love, where the harm?

The winter was our season,
It engineered the spring.
Now undergrowth has thickened,
And the nettle patch would sting.
So what's the damage, love, where the harm?

Just twice I changed the linen,
Just once you used my name,
Just once you said you loved me,
Someone else can do the same.
So what's the damage, love, where the harm?

You'll dress more lightly now,
You'll have put aside those plaids,
I've cut the hair that liked you,
I'm no longer gone on hats.
So there's no damage, love, and no harm.

The Wineglass

We can never play it back again,
Our love-life's little song and story.
The wineglass slips your fingers' hold
And signals to the planet's core.
I could, for just one millisecond,
Restore the moment to your hand.
Instead we watch it gather force
Along the curve-line through the floor.
We can never play it back again,
Our love-life's little song and story.

Make Believe

Nearly a year gone, and we're on our way home
From some museum or other, upstairs on the bus
Which the children (stop/go, rev, rev) make believe
They're driving, when there she is out of nowhere
Just like the first time, then perched side-saddle on
A sofa arm and wearing that piss-off boxer's face ...
Now rainswept, sleeveless, hugged by shopping bags,
And bantam-quick with one thin hand to bring us
To a stop halfway across Waterloo Bridge.
I say, *I'm just dropping downstairs a second*,
They both give me a look, but already we're
In motion (door-hiss, gear-change) out into traffic.

When I sat beside you and held the ashtray to
The timely avalanche of ash, all you said was *You,*
Where've you sprouted from? and *It's a ramekin!*
Then one eyebrow arched and I saw some rogue gene
Caused just one cheek to dimple: so does it now,
While she quizzes me in silence with her eyes.
You're the same, I say, which is true – except for a detail:
The same air of ironic, anglified distance,
The same snappy-odd assortment of dress,
The skin's same hint of blue undercoat – and still
Susceptible to morning bristles and polar blasts?
To eczema, to age m'dear, and Guinness?

So far, so good. As I used to say each time we'd met,
My eyes still on the space you'd slipped from,
Gone with one last twist of the head, a full swivel
While in gracile flight towards that morning's black cab
Or back up the steps to your screen and telephone,

Juggling as you went keys, pass, bag, yet managing,
In the last stride, just one look more
So that I knew when it stopped, it was over,
Knew that day, nearly a year ago, when you stalked off,
Head high, among the concert-goers and culture tourists,
When I might have shaken you by those anorexic bones
and hissed (O recalcitrant daughter/repentant wife)
Anything, anybody, just come to me now and then.

What I did say, to the restive filling auditorium,
Was *She can go* fuck *herself* – and was that, p'tite-tête,
Just what you did? Where are they, I want to whisper,
To 'whisperee' in your ear – since we're on the road once more
To the Elephant, past the kiosk where you've made the call,
And up the stairs to the arctic attic where you'll roll us
A spliff and we'll play the Jo(a)nies (Mitchell and Armatrading)
And, tongue-in-groove, we'll push off into the bruised
And orange night – where am I going in this merciful/
Lonely amplitude, *whither in my middle years?*
And where are they, I want to whisper, those winter pets,
The hamsters you kept for me in your armpits?

Why do we fall for them, the strangers whom we fall for?
As on that morning, a month after your exodus,
Days when, however I searched, I couldn't see you
Either in my real or my mind's eye, until that instant
On the ramp at Blackfriars I fell into your stride, that ball-
Of-the-foot craning gait, and your unlikely tall stem
As though perpetually slightly pissed or breeze-blown,
When it all comes back, with voice and smells and texture
Even to your dead-of-night, twice-only weight-lifter's shout
Ringing/singing in my ear, then the absolute grey dawn

When, most urgently, you whisperee *Must go, must go.*
And I hold you in the long tease of my fast embrace.

Let me hold – before you go on your self-hugging dash
Into the polar cold – your anisotropic sweet face,
Before I slide again into the infrared spoor
Of your pheromones and sweat, the cascading tiny charge
Of all you've dreamed, remembered, or obscurely planned
This last night/this year of nights with/without me,
Let me touch again your tic-douloureux,
The tender spot of your affliction, before I slip
Into my seat unnoticed, so intent are my kids
(Brake-squeak, door-hiss) in their game of make believe,
Before they set you down yards from your door, in sight
of your window: a slight, fair-haired, pretty young woman
Making off with bags from Gap, Sue Ryder, Monsoon ...
With one half-twist towards us of her dear head.

After-image

Still I see you –
white upturned face, small
in a man's duffel coat.
In how many stations
have you stood,
stood and wavered,
a stray flake in the sleety rain?

Afterthought

I see you've acquired curtains for the window. You don't
draw them.

The Schrödingers' Cat

If, as quantum theory suggests, the world only exists because it is being observed, then it is also true that the world only changes because it is not being observed all the time.

John Gribbin

That damned cat was at it again in the night.
I took one of these paperweights and let fly. It clipped
the glazed roof, then skittered off into the moonlight.
But I woke with the recollection of a thump,
a yelp, some unearthly commotion. Then silence.

It got to me round midmorning, and over I went.
The place was a haven of peace, finches and sparrows
in-and-out among the wistaria and laburnum,
the little Polo in its bay, parked askew,
and, sunning itself out on the forecourt, a red Merc.

I stood there eye level with the spy hole, my thumb
on the button, wondering should sleeping dogs lie.
And was about to press when I saw, nestled in the alpines
and all the world as though it had been chosen
and placed there, my paperweight bright with the dew.

Nugget

At Los Alamos at the time of the tests
but before the drop (itself a test)
they kept in an empty room off to the side,
in a sort of alcove, a silver-plated sphere.
Inside this was sealed the new element
that had never been on the earth – or not,
they reckoned, since near the beginning.
One could view it there through an open door.
They would sometimes warm their hands on it,
while chewing the fat with visiting brass
or shooting the breeze with some young techno,
whose attention they might eventually draw
to the chunk of gold they'd put for a doorstop.

The Sphere

Why bother with words? Geometry existed before the Creation.

Kepler

When to do so – when to imagine the world
as a sphere hanging in the heavens – meant
you belonged to a sect, Eratosthenes measured
the earth's circumference: a number that lived
through burnings and mayhem, through the centuries-long
recessions, and reached Columbus as a whisper
(who, had he trusted it, wouldn't have sailed).

It helped that Eratosthenes was Librarian
at Alexandria, that Alexandria stood
on the Nile delta, that the Nile made a straight line
due south across the sand to Syene
where – the librarian read – the noonday sun
at midsummer cast no shadow but blazed
into the well-shaft and lit it like a torch

– as if nature and history had contrived
a vast Euclidean figure, the Mouseion
(and himself) at one of its points: the basis
for a calculation that spread the map
beyond the dreams of emperors but which proved,
when the earth was viewed like a water-ball
spinning calmly in space, almost true.

Did Eratosthenes worship sun and river?
Fear the marsh elf, the gaseous bogle?
When he looked out across the harbour and saw
the water curve, the lighthouse tilt; as he stretched

and oiled the scrolls, when year after year he unfolded
the nibbled theorems, did he simply wonder?
Or see in them a shadowy signature?

Sky

the firmament sheweth His handiwork

Nothing much falls from the heavens, not in a day's walking
Or the night that follows, out here on the moors:
One shower of hail from the entirely blue, and now
The odd star-burst that we think is comet dust
Igniting in the stratosphere – but nothing like
The skillet-size snowflakes that hit Matt Coleman's ranch
In '32; neither signs nor wonders,
Neither manna nor the Welshman's *pwdre ser*,
Never mind the parachute fifty years falling on Bodmin
Or the three suns – the Sun in Splendour! – that shone
On the eve of the Battle at Mortimer's Cross;
And nothing at all to compete with the asteroid-punch,
The lumpy planetesimal plucked from the Main Belt
Or the rugby ball booted mindlessly out of the Oort Cloud
That knocked the dinosaur off its ledge – not unless we
    start to think
Of the whole shebang taking a breather, a merciful lull,
In which the biochemical soup simmers
On the cosmic hob, while an inconspicuous quadruped,
With opposable thumbs and a nocturnal habit,
Goes on a blinder – leapfrogs from prey to hunter, from
    stalking
To husbandry, as brain and pelvic cavities egg each other on
Towards this tender equilibrium, this steady state
In which our soufflé spirits rise. Where nothing falls or spills,
Or not enough to sizzle the gently smouldering mass
Or collapse the mildly stinging air into a liquid bullet
And cancel one summer's night under the stars.

Southpaw

I'm surprised, you could say a little shocked,
to find your left hand equals mine
now we're landed in this heat-struck Welsh stubble
we've jumped several hundred miles to

and it's either a split second or several months
since, on the splintering boards of your flat,
you were feeding me half-pint mickeys
of aquavit in ice-cold sips from your mouth.

You push and I ache but I hold you steady.
And I've time now to take in the boy's shoulders,
the mannish cut of the jaw, the hairline
of sweat above the lip and the metis-brown

all-over burn of your skin, time and world enough,
before we either bite or kiss, to overhear
– is it Mammy's voice from beyond the grave? –
That one, she could do with a scrub, son.

The Dinner Call
in memory

My mother comes to the doorstep
and issues her dinner call: three rising notes,
something between a yodel and a mimicked cockcrow.
I rise from the sand-heap. And I listen.
She questions me with one cupped ear.
Did we hear it, or not? A faint answering *halloo*.

My mother comes to the doorstep,
her head back, one hand shading her slant eyes,
and issues her dinner call: a sound I can hear
but cannot quite repeat – not a shout, nor yet song,
but carrying to the summery-silent fields,
to the Glens, to the Big Bog, and the Little Bog;

to my father birthing a calf; to the men
stooking barley or winding hay; to the sowers,
the reapers and the binders; to hire and help,
the vets and pole-men and drainage inspectors;
to the old dray Jack, and Billy the wild one;
to girls out blackberrying; the boys naked
in the stream; her brothers coursing a hare;
to the quiet man fencing the boundary;
to my namesake, and to my son's namesake;
to her own father ploughing the Back Field.

My mother comes to the doorstep
and issues her dinner call: three rising notes.
And the voice carries and holds.

Playing with Water
for M and N

They've made a lake in the sand
which they feed with rivers. It seeps out.
They replenish it. It goes.
Now they mix dandelions and moss
and infuse six bottles an oily green.
But these they set aside.
They make a heap of the patio dust
and sprinkle it. It becomes earth,
then mud. They squeeze it into cakes,
biscuits, a bigger cake
decorated with snail shells and buttercups.
Now the girl points the hose
While her brother holds a jug some feet away.
There must be a formula
involving *pi* for the arc
the water makes – which they've got right,
just about, but find
there's pleasure too in missing.
They aim it at the flowerpot
and the impact breaks
the sunlight into misty bands.
Studiously, then, they write their names and watch them dry.
But now they're playing apart, just pouring water,
Running it through their fingers.
They watch it splash.
After an hour or more they come inside
to show me their white hands.

Floods
late Stoic school

That the world is a watery place
was known to ancient peoples like the Sumerians
as well as to our own Ovid, and it makes sense
when you think about it: since overnight
puddles appear in the vineyard, a flash flood
uproots an oak planted in the Punic wars;
we find the oats lodged, an onager drowned,
the mullet fisher's boat upended.
True, we associate rain with these occurrences.
But it isn't what causes them, since rain
has little impact on the earth
– something you can check for yourself
if you dig the ground after a downpour:
you'll find it dry just under the sod.
Think then of great rivers: the Rhône and Danube
flowing winter and summer, year in year out,
from places where the rainfall varies
– where does all their water come from?
Now consider another phenomenon:
that the Nile, with its seven mouths, flows
into the Lower Sea, and along with it
countless lesser rivers, streams, canals, sewers,
so that large amounts of water drain
day and night off the land; yet the sea
doesn't rise nor its saltiness diminish
– a problem that baffled Aristotle,
though the explanation is simple enough.
But first, one thing more – which is the view,
favoured by the poets, that the workings
of nature are divine: thus the crofter

donates his bag of grain to Ceres,
and the pregnant girl says no to pleasure
in the hope Juno will attend the birth.
That we still practise such superstitions
is due to Virgil, a sublime and a patriotic poet,
but not a man of curious intellect.
Remember, he grew up in the North
where he had a Gaulish nurse who filled
his head with trolls and old wives' tales;
then wrote in exile, long after the farm
was lost, poems recalling country life,
so memorably he has perpetuated
among us a transcendent view of nature.
The pity is imagination obscures
the beauty of the natural world.
The truth is stranger (though no less inspiring)
than the poets believe, as in this matter of water.
Think of all of it we see around us.
Now try to picture what we do not see;
what happens under the ocean floor,
underground where the rivers originate;
how the earth has a system not unlike
our bodies, with a regulated exchange
and flow between its parts, some of it
open to sight but most hidden away;
yet there's much we can deduce by analogy:
just as we know the heart maintains a steady
pressure in the veins, making us supple
and active, buoyant venturesome creatures,
so too the earth has inner resources,
conduits wider than the Nile,
salt lakes as deep as the Black Sea;
it has pumps, filters, valves, fires,

centres of distillation and change,
which give us waters that are pure
and sweet, or bitter and sulphurous;
some that are healthy, while others kill;
waters that are hard, soft, heavy, light – so light
it forms the mysterious cirrus
that never touches the mountain top.
Now we see the earth is like a water vessel.
And if we add the quantities locked up
in ice and snow, retained in wells,
swamps, bogs, mudflats, the moisture
distributed generally in the soil
or used to make fogs and dewfall;
those tied up in trees, grass and other plants,
and in the bodies of the animals,
we see more of the world is water than isn't.
Think then of the agency of water,
how it's manipulated by the engineer
to irrigate the orchards, to turn
the miller's wheel, to give the house
plumbing and hot water; how it cools
the courtyard and ensures hygiene
at the baths, all in accordance with the rule:
water flows downhill – yet in growing things
it works its way higher than any fountain,
even to the top of the giant Lebanon cedar.
And if you step under the willow in March,
when it foams with lemony shoots,
you'll see just how like a fountain it is.
But the general principle is common
to every plant, from the marsh reed to the elm,
and explains their wind-blown restlessness.
And what are we ourselves but plants

who've pulled our feet from the earth,
so when we run, water expresses
this double nature: to rise and to flow.
Moreover water, which in its pure state
is colourless, without taste or smell,
produces just these effects in living things.
We need only think of years when the Nile
fails to flood and the land to the south
becomes a flat burnt desert.
Egypt practically ceases to exist.
But when the floods return and overrun
the dykes, they smear the bare ground
with a coat of mud, the so-called alluvium.
The soil thrives then, and brings forth
every type of vegetable and fruit.
In a matter of weeks, the earth breaks
into leaf and blossom and ripening grain.
This mud is credited with such power
the marsh women rub it in their private places
to encourage pregnancy, a primitive
and no doubt a suspect practice,
but it comes from sound intuition:
for life we know begins as a liquid
which, once it's stored inside the womb,
solidifies and undergoes changes of shape
and density, so that the child reaches term
perfectly formed but with the joints
still loose, and with a soft-boned skull
that acts, like a compressible wedge,
to force a passage through the birth canal.
Then if, by fortune and the midwife's skill,
he survives, we find he has a firm grip
and a liking for his mother's milk.

That our bodies keep their love of fluids
we know – and our health testifies,
since it requires a balance of the humours.
Even our thoughts and moods seem
to come in spurts, to dissipate, dry up;
and when, in the stress of joy and grief,
words fail, the body expresses water.
But water doesn't, like Midas' hand,
transform all at once; rather it works
along a line that cannot be erased,
and it moves in one direction only.
We can't retrieve a minute from the past.
Neither can we pre-empt the outcome
of the war, the card game, the youthful marriage.
We call this time: whose effect we tell
by the shadow on the gnomon, the ache
in the muscle, by seeing the child grow
even as we note the passing seasons.
We'll know it too by hair loss, rheumatism, death.
It's no wonder we say it 'flows'
and that poets, devising metaphors
for the ups and downs of men and cities,
have set their heroes on the water.
But time has a scale in which our lives
(and this is fortunate) appear as fluctuations;
just as the farm boy pumps the pig's bladder
to a calculated critical pressure
– so it's light and bouncy but doesn't burst –
so time maintains, below the skin of human substance,
the watery structures of the world.
But it's easier to knock down than to build,
as we learn; ten years we write the book,
ten seconds in the fire; twenty years

and the boy grows to be Adonis;
the Parthian's arrow whistles through his neck;
six centuries we construct the city,
one night in the hands of drunks or Germans;
and nature, which is methodical,
which separated out the land and drew
from it the first living creature,
then fashioned, as some suggest, a chain
linking the worms to ourselves,
knows also, believe me, how to destroy.
You have seen a torrent rush out
of the hill after a thunder storm,
as if 'a spigot has been pulled';
or you have stood on the cliff edge
and seen the ocean whipped by the wind,
and though it heaves against the sky
it scarcely bothers to paw the shore
or flick the fishing boat from its back.
What, you may ask, will happen when nature
throws off this mask – when the seas
rear heavenwards and charge inland,
while rivers come unbridled from the hills?
Will it be, as Ovid has written, men
take to their skiffs, as they did
in former times? *The strong stag's
fine long legs, growing weedier,
tangle in undercurrents; birds tire
of the air; the ocean, with nowhere else
to go, makes its bed in the hills, pulling
its coverlet over the bare summits;
and while starvation picks off a few
survivors, mankind drowns like a plague
of frogs, with imploring limbs outspread.*

It's well described. But if I've understood Thales,
Empedocles, Galen and the rest,
and if reason has informed my hand
in this the ninth year of Nero, six years
since childbirth carried off calm Lavinia,
leaving behind my son and daughter,
if my efforts have brought me to safe conclusions,
no such drawn-out spectacle occurs.
And the reason is this: that time,
in its large-scale motion, follows
neither the relentless line of Heraclitus
nor the Pythagoreans' circle turning on itself,
but the rule of the pendulum which,
as it nears one extreme, slows down
– like I've said, we've no sensible
experience of time, but just as we can say
a house-fly, resting on the weight,
is unwary of movement, so we've no notion
of our swift descent or slowing climb
except in this: as time loses momentum,
the steady metamorphic pressure fails;
the seasons hardly change, the harvests rot;
the countryside becomes deserted;
then, as people congregate, they turn
to sports and mindless travel; the brain
veers from exhilaration to depression;
and as the female voice deepens,
we drift towards androgyny;
and since women shirk motherhood,
the populace grows old; the urban fox
and then the wolf appear in this the age
of opportunity, when people thrive
on others' needs – but predation soon

gives way to lethargy, as time braces itself
and when it comes to a stop, this, we may suppose,
is the moment of flood, when the waters
shake off restraint and capsize the world;
or rather, like those wine-skins the punters
at the racetrack fling to refresh the horses
which, on impact, disintegrate and splash,
nature loses its solid manifestation.
And the world pauses, inert and featureless,
suspended in its true watery state;
until the pendulum starts in reverse,
then water resumes its temporal effect
to remake our world, or one like it; with lives like ours,
swinging rapidly between extremes.